BE STUPID

First published in the United States of America in 2011 by
Rizzoli International Publications; Inc.
300 Park Avenue South
New York, NY 10010
www.rizzoliusa.com

Originally published in Italian in 2011 by
RCS Libri S.p.A.

© 2011 RCS Libri S.p.A., Milan

All rights reserved. No part of this publication may be reproduced, stored in a retrieval system or transmitted in any form or by any means, electronic, mechanical, photocopying, recording, or otherwise, without prior written consent of the publishers.

Second printing, 2011
2011 2012 2013 2014 / 10 9 8 7 6 5 4 3 2

ISBN: 978-0-8478-3758-8

Library of Congress Control Number: 2011932312

Designed by Stefano Rossetti and Daniela Arnoldo for Pepe Nymi

The Strategy of Stupid texts by Guido Corbetta

Photography Credits
Renzo Rosso's personal archive: pp. I, II top, VIII top
Diesel's archive: pp. II bottom, III, IV, V, VI, VII, VIII bottom
The ad campaign photograph (p. IV bottom) by Ellen Von Unwerth

Every effort has been made to cite all copyrighted materials. Any inaccuracies brought to the publisher's attention will be corrected for future editions.

Printed in Italy by Grafica Veneta S.p.A. - Trebaseleghe (PD)

RENZO ROSSO

BE STUPID

for Successful Living

New York · Paris · London · Milan

CONTENTS

PREFACE by *Guido Corbetta*   9
VARIOUS REASONS FOR BEING STUPID   13

/01 SMART SEES WHAT THERE IS.
    STUPID SEES WHAT THERE COULD BE.   16

/02 SMART CRITIQUES. STUPID CREATES.   24

/03 IF YOU'VE NEVER DONE ANYTHING STUPID,
    YOU'VE NEVER DONE ANYTHING AT ALL.   32

/04 SMART LISTENS TO THE HEAD.
    STUPID LISTENS TO THE HEART.   40

/05 STUPID MIGHT FAIL.
    SMART DOESN'T EVEN TRY.   48

/06 IN STUPID WE TRUST.   56

/07 ONLY THE STUPID CAN BE TRULY BRILLIANT.   64

    FRIENDS/01   76

/08 SMART PLANS. STUPID IMPROVISES.   80

/09 SMART MAY HAVE THE BRAINS,
   BUT STUPID HAS THE BALLS.   88

/10 BE STUPID. THERE'S NO WRONG WAY TO DO IT.   96

/11 SMART HAD ONE GOOD IDEA, AND THAT WAS STUPID. 104

/12 SMART SAYS NO. STUPID SAYS YES.   112

   FRIENDS/02   120

/13 ARE YOU SMART ENOUGH TO BE STUPID?   124

/14 STUPID IS TRIAL AND ERROR.
   MOSTLY ERROR.   132

/15 HELLO STUPID. GOODBYE PANTS.   140

   FRIENDS/03   148

/16 BE STUPID. YOU'LL MAKE MORE FRIENDS   152

/17 BE STUPID. YOU'LL CREATE MORE.   160

/18 BE STUPID. YOU'LL NEVER WANT TO BE ANYWHERE ELSE. 170

   FAMILY   180

   STUPID IS GOOD FOR YOU.   184

   Conclusion   189

   Acknowledgments   192

PREFACE
Guido Corbetta
Professor of Corporate Strategy
Bocconi University, Milan

I cannot hide my fondness for entrepreneurs, for people who risk what they have in order to chase a dream that comes straight from the heart. I admire their determination, their willingness to work hard, their ability to stay a step ahead of everyone else, their commitment to never playing it safe and accepting the possibility of failure. I like them because they make real contributions to improving the world in which we live.

Renzo Rosso is a true entrepreneur, who, in a little over thirty years, has created an international company, and in an area Americans once seemed destined to dominate forever. He achieved this through trial and error, all based on his conviction that "playing it safe doesn't lead to innovation, while risk leads to evolution." This book contains many episodes that illustrate his philosophy, and I'm sure each reader will focus on something different. One thing I found "brilliantly stupid" was the idea of accepting a high-profile advertising award in Cannes by going onstage with four people who worked for him, each of whom wore a rubber mask of Rosso's face. I can only imagine how impressed the four of them, and the audience, were by his generosity in sharing the award—an act that tells you everything you need to know about building a community of motivated and determined people to achieve even the most ambitious goals.

Renzo Rosso isn't literally stupid; he doesn't fit the dictionary definition of a person who "possesses or reveals very low intelligence." But the word "stupid" is of Latin origin, and it's related to the verb "to stupefy." So it seems clear to me why Rosso writes, "in the future, when the 'Be Stupid' ad campaign is over, the philosophy that inspired it will remain inscribed in Diesel's DNA." His is a philosophy that aims to teach people to be amazed by what happens and to stupefy others. If we aren't amazed, everything becomes banal, been-there-done-that routine. The things that stupefy us aren't necessarily pleasant, but if they're used in an intelligently provocative way, they can touch our hearts and minds and help us think about sensitive social issues.

Renzo Rosso has handed down this philosophy to his six children.

The letter from three of them (Andrea, Stefano, and Alessia) included in this publication stands as a grateful tribute to their family. They have been raised with basic, simple values paired with "a unique, international, and open-minded way of seeing the world, irreverently and with a strong sense of humor—in short, stupid!"

And like their father, they also had a "brilliantly stupid" idea: to celebrate the Diesel brand's thirtieth anniversary by offering fans around the world the company's core product at a heavily discounted price for one day.

One of the great secrets to the success of family-run companies is just that ability to build on the values that comprise their legacy in a new way. Renzo Rosso has taught this philosophy not just to his children, but also to the people who work for him. This book is full of designers, ad agencies, and many others who have pushed themselves "to the edge . . . without falling," and who have learned to be amazed and to amaze. With this book, Renzo Rosso aims to speak to the many potential readers, illustrating the philosophy on which his success as an entrepreneur is based. Each business story is specific, and success is always the result of a totally personal combination of factors, and yet it seems to me that in these pages readers will find an important truth without which an entrepreneur cannot be born or grow: at times, decisions must be made that normal companies may find stupid.

Would you open your first store in the United States in New York City, right across the street from your main competition? Renzo Rosso did, and it was a great success.

Guido Corbetta

VARIOUS REASONS FOR BEING STUPID

Diesel has run many ad campaigns. Each campaign has, at least in part, expressed the essence of this brand: sexy, provocative, eccentric, ironic, at times bewildering, though always fun and careful never to underestimate people's intelligence.

One day, however, we launched a campaign with the tagline "Be Stupid." The idea was simple: to transform our way of working and thinking into a manifesto. "Be Stupid" means doing anything reasonable people tell you not to do: be bold, be daring, push yourself to the limit, break the rules, follow your instinct and your heart, do something because you like doing it and don't worry when people warn you about the consequences.

It was a great idea, and it deeply touched fans of our brand and creative people around the world.

I soon realized that "Be Stupid" was more than a mere ad campaign: like another slogan of ours, "For Successful Living," it perfectly captured the spirit of our company. "Be Stupid" is more than a slogan; it's what we are.

"Be Stupid" is an empowering philosophy. In everything we do, we should ask ourselves if the stupidity factor is high enough. Are we really being bold enough to have an impact on the market? Or are we compromising?

Since I believe in sharing, I decided to write a short book about the "Be Stupid" concept and the history of Diesel. Here, you'll read about some of our decisive moments and see that very often we've made decisions that normal companies would no doubt consider stupid. What have we learned from these experiences? And what conclusions can others draw?

In the pages that follow, you'll find anecdotes about me and my friends, my colleagues, and even my family. The chapter titles are all taken from the "Be Stupid" ad campaign.

As company founder, and the person who is responsible for the careers of so many other people, I refuse to be stupid without a valid reason. Diesel and its corporate group, Only The Brave, are independent: I don't have to answer to any nerve-wracked shareholders. But I respect my coworkers too much to put their jobs at risk. All I ask is that they push themselves as close to the edge as possible, without falling.

I humbly offer you this book, *Be Stupid*. I hope you find in it the colorful story of our company, a starting point for a new ideology, and, of course, some pleasant reading.

Enjoy,

Renzo R.
xxx

SMART SEES WHAT THERE IS. STUPID SEES WHAT THERE COULD BE.

/01

Renzo and the Rabbits

SMART SEES WHAT THERE IS. STUPID SEES WHAT THERE COULD BE.

Not many people know that I grew up on a farm. I'm proud of my roots and the down-to-earth way I was raised (and taught what really matters in life, such as respect for others and dignity).

My parents' farm was—and still is—in Brugine, a small town in the lower Po Valley, a little over sixty miles (one hundred kilometers) from where the Diesel headquarters stand today. The area was far from wealthy at the time. The town had only two television sets (one in a bar and the other in the church sacristy) and one car that served two thousand people. One of the funniest stories from my childhood is very revealing in terms of my future career. I loved being outdoors, but I also loved studying with my friends. My friend Walter, who was always at the top of the class and a great guy, gave me one of the rabbits his father raised. He probably intended for the animal to be cooked and eaten, but I was so fascinated by the breeding process that I had him explain all his father's techniques to me. A few days later I discovered the rabbit was female, and pregnant! I went to buy some chicken wire fencing, and I used a pair of pliers to build a few small cages with a rudimentary food and water system for the rabbits (basically, I cut up some plastic bottles and installed them upside down). In a year and a half, I must have raised 150 rabbits. About half I kept and bred, while I sold the others each month at the market I visited with my father.

I can just picture myself: a small boy in a grown-up world, determined to sell his rabbits to the highest bidder. I had a sales strategy, which consisted of stressing that my rabbits had been raised completely naturally. The result?

At the age of twelve, I was already a professional breeder.

Then something clicked. All of a sudden I saw my future! From that first business experience, I learned that if you had a good product and were willing to work hard and be patient, you could make some money.

The rabbit episode came to mind a few years later, when I discovered an even better product.

But that's another story.

The Strategy of Stupid

Knowing a person's history, his past, helps you understand him in the present.

If you live on a farm, if you have parents who teach you basic, practical values, if you don't waste time watching too much TV (even if it's because television sets aren't a common sight), if you have generous classmates who give you rabbits and you find someone who's willing to explain how to raise them, there's a good chance you'll get involved in selling rabbits for food. But that's not enough.

You also need to experience the flash of brilliance that shows you an alternative to just eating the rabbit right away. You need to be curious enough to ask how to raise them, and intelligent enough to listen carefully to the answers. You need the manual skill to build rabbit hutches. You need to be patient enough to wait for them to grow and naively courageous enough to try and sell your products on the "grown-up" market.

In short, entrepreneurs have the ability to "see" an opportunity for innovation and to act on it, alone or with others. Business opportunities are all around us. Entrepreneurs are just people who are "ready, willing, *and able," and who indefatigably dedicate themselves to seeking out these possibilities.*

There's luck involved, as well. If the rabbit Walter gave his friend Renzo Rosso had been male, would the story have gone differently? Maybe yes, because no rabbit breeding business would have gotten off the ground. But then the "stupid/stupefied" boy he was would have looked for other outlets for his entrepreneurial spirit. And, in fact, that's exactly what happened.

My stupid ideas

SMART CRITIQUES.
STUPID CREATES.
/02

Dangerous Denim

When I was young, nothing made a father prouder than seeing his children get a formal education. I was the youngest of three, and my two older siblings had decided not to take the academic route. Growing up, I started to consider various possibilities. By the time I was a teenager, like almost all teenagers, I cared about three things: music (I played electric guitar in a band), my looks (an important way of broadcasting your personality), and girls (not necessarily in that order—girls were actually at the top of the list). I heard about a school in Padua, the Istituto Marconi—today it's called Istituto Natta—that offered a curriculum for becoming a manufacturing consultant. It was a new and experimental course of study—the only one of its kind in Italy—and rather than full-time professors, the teachers were people who worked in the many textile companies located in our region. They would talk inspiringly about what went on behind the scenes in the fashion world. To be honest, I chose the school because it was considered "easy," which was stupid, but it sparked my imagination.

I started out studying industrial patterns (how to make them) and attending workshops (how to cut cloth and assemble the pieces). I even took down notes from a lecture on how to make a shirt and shared them. If I'm not mistaken, they're still circulating today at the school!

One day, a friend who worked in the textile industry got me several meters of real denim imported from the United States, and I knew immediately what I wanted to do with it. Using the few things I had learned at school at that point, I made a pattern. Then, I borrowed my mother's sewing machine. With great enthusiasm, I made my first garment, something really original: a pair of tight-fitting bellbottom pants, with a 42-cm flare and a low waistline. (It was the 1970s!) No one had ever seen anything like them in my neck of the woods.

I was fifteen, and I had made my first pair of jeans.

Of course, they weren't perfect. For example, there was a problem with the zipper: I had neglected to sew a strip of fabric behind the zipper, so every time I zipped them up, I went into a cold sweat, dreading the possibility of a painful accident. I'm still not sure where I got this stupid idea, but the denim I used to make the pants was uncomfortably stiff, so I rubbed them on some concrete in our yard. I may have inadvertently invented distressed denim right then and there.

The jeans were a big hit: all my friends wanted some. I charged 3,500 lire a pair, less than 1.80 euro today, to cover the cost of labor and materials. Soon my room was full of patterns. I made them for all my friends, real custom-made items. I'm not sure how many I ended up making. Somewhere around thirty, although it seemed like hundreds to me at the time.

I discovered tailoring, fashion, a world in which I had no background and no pedigree . . . but above all, I discovered denim. Since then I've never looked back.

The Strategy of Stupid

Renzo Rosso's friend Walter gave him a rabbit. A few years later, another friend gave him several yards of real denim imported from the United States, and yet more friends asked him to make them pants.

A question naturally comes to mind: Why did Rosso have so many friends? Maybe because he didn't brag about how smart he was. Maybe because he didn't criticize others. Maybe because he played the electric guitar (well?). Maybe because he was good-looking.

I'm not sure of the answer, but I know that a stupid person first creates a network of friends and builds relationships based on respect. This is the essential difference between an inventor and an entrepreneur: an entrepreneur has to work with and for others—be they clients, coworkers, or suppliers.

An entrepreneur has to create a product that satisfies an existing need in an innovative way. Rosso's story teaches us that in order to innovate, you need to immerse yourself in your surroundings and be alert to their potential: school, your mother's sewing machine, the opinions of those who influence purchases—girls, in this case—parties to display your product and get feedback, your bedroom as both workshop and warehouse.

The stupid person isn't made happy by criticizing something or someone (teachers are boring; mom's sewing machine is old; my bedroom's too small); instead, he's made happy by seeing the beauty of what comes from his head and his hands.

One question remains: why did he charge only 3,500 lire?

My stupid ideas

IF YOU'VE NEVER DONE ANYTHING STUPID, YOU'VE NEVER DONE ANYTHING AT ALL.
03/

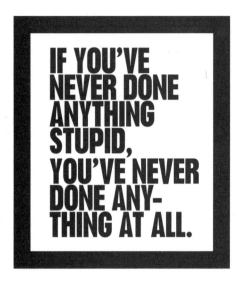

How to (Almost) Get Yourself Fired

I was lucky to have a great mentor: Adriano Goldschmied. Unfortunately, things got off on the wrong foot between us. When I finished school, I found a job at Moltex, a company Adriano owned that made the most popular jeans on the market at that time: Daily Blue. When I interviewed for the job, I wasn't completely honest: I didn't tell them that in a few short months I'd have to perform my compulsory military service, and I lied, claiming that I had work experience when really all I'd done was study the industry in a classroom. I had to oversee eighteen people working on the production line. I knew a fair amount about the industry in general, but only in theory. In practice, I was faced with eighteen machine workers with their equipment and a stock of cut garments ready to be assembled. It was a shock. I had no idea where to start. Panic stricken, I phoned a friend who had done the same kind of work, and I asked him, "What should I do?"

It was like a scene in a movie where a passenger is forced to land an airplane and stays on the line with the control tower the whole time.

I must have called him twenty times, every twenty minutes. That evening I stopped by his home, and I spent the whole night there, desperately trying to gather the information that would allow me to pull this off.

The first week was pretty problematic because I wasn't able to produce a single pair of jeans, but luckily my boss was out of the country! Finally, slowly, things got better, and toward the end of the month I started getting the hang of it. Taking the job was a risky move for sure, but then again, I had so little to lose, and I knew that, somehow, I would make it work. When I feel strongly about something, I go for it—all the way. If you stick your neck out, you'll often find luck comes your way because eventually I found out that I wouldn't have to do military service after all. The government decided to call up only 50 percent of the eligible men born after 1955. The number fifty-five has always brought me luck!

I stayed at that job for two and a half years, and eventually I ended up resting on my laurels. I was twenty years old, loved life, loved women. Work—well, I loved that a little less. I lost focus and production started to decline.

One evening Adriano invited me to his home for dinner, along with some other guests. At one point he called me into his study and said, "I like you, and you definitely have what it takes, but you don't want to work hard. You're fired." I was stunned. I begged and pleaded. "I'll show you how hard I can work," I promised.

Fortunately, Adriano's wife, Rossella, was very fond of me, and she persuaded him to give me a second chance. Come to think of it, women have always brought me luck, too! Adriano had a good idea: he offered me a performance-based bonus.

I would earn X for a small increase in production, Y for substantial growth, and Z for an enormous, almost impossible-to-achieve level of growth. It was good motivation for me. If you tell me I can't do something, I'll push myself to the limit to show you you're wrong.

The first month I immediately reached level Z: my salary jumped from 240,000 lire to 2,400,000 lire, and that's how it went for three months. The fear of being fired, combined with the "impossible" goal, drove me and made me see that I could achieve something great on my own. That's when I told Adriano, "Thanks a lot—but now I'm quitting."

> **IF YOU'VE NEVER DONE ANYTHING STUPID, YOU'VE NEVER DONE ANYTHING AT ALL.**

The Strategy of Stupid

Applying for a job without any experience isn't reasonable. Resting on your laurels (at age twenty!) after only two years in the workplace doesn't seem reasonable. Risking getting fired doesn't seem reasonable. These things don't seem reasonable to people who are so presumptuous that they think they know how things will turn out before they even get started. Like many top entrepreneurs, Renzo Rosso isn't afraid of losing his job because he has confidence in his skills and is convinced he'll always find another one.

But maybe Rosso wouldn't have become what he is today if he didn't have a great mentor who chose him from among the new graduates (I suspect he realized that Rosso didn't have the extensive experience he claimed), who understood that Rosso was resting on his laurels, who listened to his very intelligent wife, and who gave Rosso a second chance, offering the perfect incentive. A mentor who knew how to look into the hearts of others, as only the stupid can.

Rosso was still at the start of his career and, as he writes, "Taking the job was a risky move for sure, but then *again, I had so little to lose."* This is one of the secrets of ongoing entrepreneurial success: entrepreneurs act as if they have little to lose because if you let fear of losing predominate, then you're on the defense rather than on the offense, preservation takes the place of innovation, and sooner or later decline sets in.

My stupid ideas

SMART LISTENS TO THE HEAD.
STUPID LISTENS TO THE HEART.
/04

The First of the Italian Mohicans

"Don't leave, Renzo. We need you." I could hardly believe it. Adriano Goldschmied, who just a few months earlier had almost fired me for my laziness, was now begging me to stay. I hesitated because I wanted to make it on my own, but he convinced me, offering me a 40 percent stake in Moltex, which then became a new company with a new brand: Diesel. It was October 6, 1978. I liked the name Diesel because it was short, international, and it was pronounced the same way almost everywhere in the world. Also, this was during the oil crisis, and diesel, more economical than gasoline, was the true alternative energy at the time. Plus, diesel fuel let you go farther, albeit more slowly. I adored the name, but many people didn't. They argued that it was an industrial word that connoted dirt and that it had nothing to do with jeans. I had a moment of doubt, thinking they might be right. But my job was to sell the brand. Things moved slowly, though, and we couldn't drum up support for the product. So I had an idea: we'd give that name a signature logo.

At the time I met a British artist named David who lived in Italy but was planning to move home soon because he had run out of money. Adriano said to me, "Maybe you could work with him. He's a really creative person." I met with David in Milan, looked at his portfolio, and decided to entrust him with the task of designing Diesel's logo. We agreed on his fee, and his move to Molvena, where our headquarters were located. I advanced him the price of a round-trip ticket to London: he had to go and pack some things to bring back to Italy. On the day he was supposed to return, I went to the Venice airport to pick him up, but he didn't show up. There were no cell phones back then. I figured that was it and I'd never see him again. Three days later, at two in the morning, the police phoned me. They said they had found an Englishman sleeping in a telephone booth in Marostica, many miles from Venice. He didn't speak Italian, but kept repeating three words: "Renzo. Rosso. Diesel."

    A smart person would have steered clear of someone like that, but I admired his talent, and my instinct told me that we were going to accomplish something great together. I invited him to stay with me while he designed the Diesel logo. At the time, a lot of denim brands tried to develop an American image, choosing names inspired by American Indians: Sioux, Apache, Cheyenne, and so on. I asked David to go along with that trend but to approach it from a newer, more innovative, modern, and above all original perspective. That's always been my guiding principle: taking existing things and evolving them into something different, something new. David locked himself in his room for two weeks. I had meals taken up to him, but he refused to show me any preliminary sketches. I started to worry. In the end he came out of his room and showed me a perfect India ink drawing. It was the head of an American Indian; but not just any American Indian—this was a punk Indian, a Mohican. He said, "This is your modern, metropolitan American Indian, who lives under the bridges in London." I was crazy about that logo, and I put it on every label and all sorts of clothing, starting with T-shirts. It quickly became widely known, and even today, after thirty years, it remains an iconic Diesel image.

The Strategy of Stupid

Stupid doesn't look for novelty, doesn't change for the sake of changing. Instead, stupid prefers "taking existing things and evolving them into something different, something new." Renzo Rosso accepted his mentor's offer and stayed on at the company, becoming a partner. Maybe it would have been smarter to establish a company that he could control 100 percent, but why give up working with a person your heart tells you is a friend and good businessman? It's better to stay together and launch a totally new brand.

Your head may tell you that you need to come up with a brand name directly related to jeans, to clothing. But a brand is an entrepreneur's signature, so if you like Diesel—even though its sounds dirty and industrial—you have to listen to your heart and go for it. But stupid keeps a sharp eye out, assessing whether the brand penetrates people's hearts. Do people like it? If they don't, or if they like it less than you expected, you need to do something, like launch a signature logo.

Stupid takes risks, but stupid doesn't gamble. The concept of American Indians was being used, successfully, to sell jeans around the world. Rosso didn't need to gamble on a whole new concept, when people already *associated jeans with American Indians; instead, he looked for someone capable of bringing the image up-to-date. And he did this with the key contribution of a person someone reasonable would probably have dismissed. Here again, if you like a person, if he makes an impression on you, why listen to your head? Give it a shot. After all, what have you got to lose?*

My stupid ideas

STUPID MIGHT FAIL. SMART DOESN'T EVEN TRY.
/05

Solo Flight

The nascent Diesel quickly moved up a gear and began to show early signs of success. At that time, I, along with Adriano, was part of a company that owned several other brands, such as King Jeans, Replay, Viavai, and Martin Guy. But I decided to drop the other companies and concentrate on Diesel. So in 1985, I asked Adriano if he would sell me his shares in the brand. He didn't hesitate because he'd never been fond of it, and at that point it didn't seem particularly promising. Diesel was like a child to me, though. I was ready to nurture it.

First, though, I needed financing. Investors, including banks, helped me because I had always been committed and punctual in my business relationships, despite my somewhat ragtag appearance. I was ready for anything, even failure, and I figured in the worst-case scenario I'd just run off to a deserted island. So I took a risk with considerable financing and large volumes. Immediately, sales jumped from 3.5 million euro to 8 million euro. How did I pull it off?

That's a good question. Up until 1985 I'd just been responsible for managing the brand, but now I owned it and could make exactly the product I wanted. As I was convinced that I was going to go bankrupt in less than a year, I decided to indulge all my crazy ideas—including my passion for vintage jeans.

I said to myself: "Why don't we make jeans that look used?" This was a completely new innovation: "distressing" jeans, breaking them in so that they looked like old miners' pants.

Our distributors thought we were crazy, especially since we were trying to sell the jeans as if they were works of art. Our prices were much higher than those of the competition because the treatment was expensive. It was difficult to find stores that believed in our product. I chose some business partners suited to my hypothetical customers, but I also had to work with buyers who weren't so sure about the idea: they considered the rips in the jeans defects. (It was around that time that the *Wall Street Journal* wrote, more or less, "How can this guy even think about selling jeans in their native country at twice the going rate?") But I was willing to try anything. What I wanted was to reach customers, so I made distributors an offer that was hard to refuse: take some, and if you don't sell them, I'll buy them back. Fortunately, the jeans sold like hotcakes, and from then on buyers never stopped asking for more.

I had bet on the fact that if jeans connoisseurs were willing to pay a fortune for secondhand pairs, then they would also pay a lot for new jeans that looked old. My intuition, which could be traced all the way back to my father's farm, was right. I didn't think Diesel would become a worldwide success overnight, but it was developing a cult following in a number of countries. My escape to a deserted island was put on the back burner.

The Strategy of Stupid

Seeking success in business is like riding a bicycle uphill. You gauge your passage by noting specific landmarks, but as you climb, the risk increases because you don't know what lies ahead. At a certain point, there are only two alternatives: stop to enjoy the view or keep pedaling, despite the obstacles, until you reach the top.

In 1961, David McClelland, an expert in motivational psychology, theorized that a businessman's motivation to keep challenging himself stems from his ambition to be acknowledged as someone who has made a decisive contribution to the history of his family, of a certain place, or of a specific sector. Renzo Rosso has that ambition and, in fact, he doesn't just get over the hurdles in his path; he gets over them using radical innovation provided by his own instinct. "Distressing jeans, breaking them in so that they looked like old miners' pants." The more radical the innovation, the more the stupid businessman must be prepared to risk, and he does so happily in search of his goal.

Rosso also tells us that during this phase it was relatively easy to find support from banks and suppliers despite his appearance (of course, being on time with his *payments helped)*. There's a photo of the young founders of Microsoft wearing long hair and outdated clothes. You can't help asking yourself when you look at it whether you would have invested in them. Suppliers and banks, too, must be ready to take risks. In return, those who invested in Microsoft and those who believed in Renzo Rosso were rewarded with an opportunity to participate in two great success stories.

My stupid ideas

IN STUPID WE TRUST. /06

Life on Planet Diesel

I still live in Bassano del Grappa, in the Veneto region, a very lovely ancient city nestled among the hills. Diesel was born and grew up here alongside me.

Everyone asks the same question: "Why didn't you locate your headquarters in Milan or another big city, where you'd have your pick of experienced people to hire?" The answer is simple: it's not for me. The Bassano area is where I found my first job, where my career and life have their roots.

But there's another reason: I'm convinced that this setting stimulates creativity. It's almost surreal to see so many cool and brilliant people, from all over the world, living here in the countryside. It helps to create a true community spirit. When I hire someone, I always tell him or her, "You'll like the workplace." And that's really true: everyone likes it.

These people are my work family, my team. There isn't just one "creative genius" behind Diesel's products. We're a close-knit and visionary group called the Diesel Creative Team. We constantly travel around the world looking for inspiration, and I believe that living here helps us keep our eyes open because when we travel everything seems new. We want to see, hear, understand, experience, interpret. Living here makes me a better traveler, and the same holds true for my team.

Do you want to know where they come from?

Today I choose employees differently than I used to. Back then, I would go to trade fairs in Paris and would look for creative brands that inspired me. Then I would contact the people who had worked on those collections.

I've never tried to win over star designers: I've always looked for the number two or number three person. I want young people, hungry people with a drive to reach the top and no fear of failure. And I've always pushed them to be daring. Since 2000 we've hired new designers through a truly unique system: we are a founding partner of ITS (International Talent Support) competitions.

Each year the organizers of the ITS fashion competition receive thousands of portfolios from young designers and students poised to graduate from schools around the world. After a rigorous preselection process, we invite twenty-five of the top candidates to travel to Trieste, where they present their collections to an international jury. One is selected to win the Diesel Award. The winner receives a cash prize, but more importantly, has the opportunity to spend six months with us, learning what goes into developing a collection and also about industrial manufacturing. Some of the winners have even ended up working for us.

I like young designers because they are pure: their creativity is virginal. They aren't afraid to take risks because they haven't been brainwashed about what they should or shouldn't do. They haven't become slaves to the industrial process.

By supporting projects like this one, we've created a network of Diesel friends around the world who are in some way grateful to us for what they are today.

The Strategy of Stupid

Each step in the process of creating a new entrepreneurial formula—with the exception, maybe, of businesses based on craftsmanship—involves a certain number of people with different forms of expertise and different levels of experience. That's why a leading businessman needs to know how to create a community of people, both inside and outside the company, who are motivated to take part in the entrepreneur's dream and contribute to making it come true. Many case studies prove that an entrepreneur can be judged by the quality of the people around him. Undeniably, even top Italian companies still have a lot to learn when it comes to identifying and motivating good workers. Diesel is a standard bearer in this area. Renzo Rosso offers some precious advice:

- Look for the number twos who are still hungry because they have goals to achieve
- Look for people anywhere in the world, without prejudice about their geographic locations
- Use unconventional methods, like the Diesel Award, to identify talent
- Don't rely on a single brilliant mind (in design, production, or commerce); that way you'll avoid flattening out the company to his or her level

- *Create a work environment with a sense of family or community because that's where people do their best work*
- *Push everyone to travel the world with a humble attitude—there's always more to learn*

My stupid ideas

ONLY THE STUPID CAN BE TRULY BRILLIANT. /07

The Art of Communication

Our brand is famous for communication. At this point in our story I had a high-quality product and business partners who believed in me—and who sold everything I gave them. Now I knew that I could go further. Diesel represented a lifestyle, and I felt that as many people as possible should hear about it. The time had come to communicate.

As is often the case in my life, and in the life of my company, I started from scratch, without any real knowledge of this world, but with a clear vision and a group of people full of enthusiasm and willingness to innovate. The first outside partner we found in the advertising field was a small, unknown Swedish agency. Why that one? Sheer chance. Our distributor in Sweden, Johan Lindeberg, introduced us to the people at Paradiset, who immediately grabbed our attention. They showed us a series of ad campaigns for young fashion brands, but they cleverly hid the logos. The ads were all the same. Without the logos, you couldn't tell one from the other. They were all black-and-white, gloomy, pretentious, and depressing. Immediately, we agreed that our campaign needed to be completely different! Colorful, clever, surreal images. We wanted the people who saw our ads to understand that we respected their intelligence: everyone knew we were trying to sell something, but why not also offer entertainment and food for thought (which would reach only those who wanted it and were looking for it), social commentary, rebellion?

Today, when ads for everything from cars to drugs employ irony, this probably doesn't sound like anything special. But you can't imagine the effect it had on the fashion industry ("Are they poking fun at themselves instead of praising and highlighting their products?") and the marketing industry ("Can fashion advertising offer concepts and stories?"). We even turned the idea of advertising itself on its head by offering print ads and commercials that seemed to promote everything *but* our own products (tires, hair spray, stain removers). We called the campaign series "For Successful Living," obviously a parody of the promises of success and eternal happiness used to sell you anything and everything.

While all this innovation was incredible, we had to come to terms with the fact that we had little money. Once again, a limitation became a motivation that spurred us to try to do our best. It would have been simple to make a so-so campaign and repeat it millions of times until consumers were numb to it; it was more "stupid" to make a strong, creative campaign that wouldn't pass unnoticed. We started choosing media partners, looking for the ones that were most in sync with us. We were among the first fashion brands to buy advertising in gay magazines (*Out*) and magazines on the emerging digital world (*Wired*).

We chose magazines based on our own taste ("Would I buy this magazine?") rather than listening to annoying research and target analysis, demographic data, press runs, and so on. This is also how we picked MTV. It was the early 1990s. We were small, we wanted to grow, and we loved music. And the group of fans who had come up with the idea of the first channel dedicated to music really inspired us. For many years they they were our exclusive TV commercial partner because we shared a target audience—and because once we had paid them we had nothing left to spend.

Advertising wasn't the only weapon we used to explain to the world who we were: special mention must be made of our parties. Where could you see other people like yourself, fans of the brand? Where could you see the lifestyle we were talking about? At the events Diesel organized around the world! We started throwing unforgettable parties, many of them closely tied to the themes of our ad campaigns.

I remember the parties we threw around the world in 2001 for the "Save Yourself" campaign, which made fun of the pursuit of eternal youth with messages such as "drink urine," "inhale oxygen," and "believe in reincarnation." The party venues became enormous "workshops." While guests danced and had fun, they'd see these absurd practices coming to life: the beer taps looked like urinals; oxygen masks hung above the bar counter. One event in Paris at the Louvre (just imagine how shocked the museum's security people were when they saw how we "violated" the place) was particularly legendary. But we ended up canceling the event in New York, as the party had been planned for that fateful September 11.

Then there were our sponsorships. Instead of throwing money away to put our logo on skiers, TV programs, and whatever else, we decided that the projects we supported had to say something about who we were and our philosophy.

One day my team asked me, "What do you hope to be remembered for in fifty years' time?"

I replied, "As someone who gave talented young people a chance as it happened to me many years ago. They could be the best version of themselves if they got a little help."

We looked at our sponsorships as an opportunity to act as patrons of the arts. We found budding musicians and allowed them to play live in incredible places and to record their music. We supported new designers and helped them to show their creations to the international press and sell them in our stores. We handed over entire walls in some of the world's largest cities to emerging artists from all over the globe.

But the party of all parties, the mother of all Diesel events, the one that showed the world what we are capable of and what our principles are, took place on our thirtieth anniversary. We didn't want to repeat something we had already done and just throw a huge party with famous artists and VIPs in one of the world's fashion capitals. Once again, we pursued a stupid dream.

Diesel is a brand that belongs to the whole world, and it wouldn't have been fair to celebrate in just one place, so we decided to throw parties in seventeen different locations (this also showed that we aren't superstitious because the number seventeen is unlucky in Italy). Seventeen cities across the globe, from Tokyo to New York, all on the same day, in different time zones, all connected live in that neutral and magical place we call the Internet.

These massive events were for our fans, not just for a select few. The performers were top names like M.I.A., Kanye West, Pharrell Williams, Chaka Khan, and Earth, Wind & Fire, but also many of the young musicians Diesel has discovered over the years, through its project Diesel:U:Music, who found themselves performing in front of an audience of eighty thousand people and a virtual audience of millions.

My children also had the brilliant idea that we should be more generous than ever before to the many Diesel fans around the world. What could be more stupid than offering them a product (our core product—jeans) at a heavily discounted price, for one day, in Diesel stores all over the planet?

There were a lot of questions. What message would this product send? How would we handle the logistics? Would it sell? But the stupid voice inside of us prevailed. I remember the feeling—the tears—when messages began to pour in from country after country, in different time zones: "There's been a line in front of the store since three in the morning." "It's crazy. We had to call the police, we might have to close the shop." "We blocked all traffic in the neighborhood." "Sold out. We sold everything, there are kids crying in front of the store because they didn't get a pair of jeans."

These are unforgettable memories, and the message we gave the world was clear: we are stupid and we have a lot of friends.

The Strategy of Stupid

Communications should be creative. Experience tells us that this often isn't the case. Advertising, sponsorship, and the events promoted by various companies are frequently repeats that don't display any innovation, one just like the next.

In this area, too, you need to take risks to reap reward.

A young (not only chronologically) company often has a taste for risk. That, along with a clear vision of what to communicate, a commitment to coming up with truly unforgettable material, the willingness to make space for young people around the world—be they artists or musicians or your own children—the ability to make people reflect, and (maybe) the limited means at its disposal allowed Diesel to create a community of supporters and customers, not to mention becoming a style icon.

Obviously, not every project can be a roaring success, and a few have stirred a commotion, but what's important is that Diesel has tried to create an original style of communication by risking its own resources and its own reputation, staying ahead of the curve and anticipating trends.

One question has driven Renzo Rosso and it's a question all entrepreneurs should ask themselves: What do you hope to be remembered for in fifty years' time?

My stupid ideas

FRIENDS/01

Renzo Rosso/Rolls-Royce

Since I was a child, I've known that two overlapping Rs are a symbol of wealth and status. They represent a glamorous and perhaps unattainable world. Those overlapping Rs stand for "Rolls-Royce."

The two Rs that stand for "Renzo Rosso" represent the exact opposite. Renzo has nothing to do with the conventional and the commonplace.

Renzo is a rarity, the kind of person whose talent and determination come in a package that may look messy and maybe even a bit mad. But that's misleading. If he sometimes appears slightly mad, it's only because he's always ahead of his time.

Renzo knows how to see the future, know what's coming, and wrangle it to serve his needs—like a skilled cowboy.

Now that I think of it, he even looks like someone who lives on the plains and forges through the frontier. On first contact, you see him as messy, but that's only because we're conditioned to see successful entrepreneurs as specific types.

My friend Renzo knows how to laugh and how to make others laugh.

We laugh so much at ourselves, always with that simplicity that only people of great human character exhibit.

I remember once Renzo and I were getting on a private jet—a great symbol of privilege and exclusivity—to travel to Romania. He broke all the rules by making everyone get out of their comfortable leather seats and squat down on the floor. Then he opened his knapsack—the kind a young backpacker carries—and he withdrew an enormous piece of Grana Padano cheese, a salami—which he claimed to have cured himself—some toasted bread, and a lovely bottle of wine. *Rosso,* or red, naturally.

The mood changed in an instant. We spent the rest of the trip alternately laughing and listening to his predictions of the future. I still recall every word of those "mad" visions of his.

Renzo is passionate about many things, including wine. An art connoisseur and collector, his ability to anticipate the next big thing serves him well as he seeks out young talent around the world and asks for his inspiration to be translated into concrete form.

He likes to feel "stupid," in the sense of thinking outside of the box and remaining free and independent.

So I, too, want to be as stupid as my friend RR, who shares his initials and little else with Rolls-Royce. In our country—indeed, in our beloved Veneto region—he has gathered young, talented individuals and let them dream as they are challenged. He has given them a company known and loved around the world.

Renzo, being your friend makes me stupid, too.

Gratefully yours,

Roberto Baggio
World Cup Soccer Legend

SMART PLANS. STUPID IMPROVISES. /08

Pruning Encourages New Growth

One day I announced that we were going to trim our distribution network by eliminating two thousand stores. Needless to say, everyone thought I was crazy, and the CEO wanted to kill me.

Here's the story: by the mid-1990s, Diesel had grown so much that it was distributed around the world through many different stores, both big and small, luxury and mainstream. In order to stand out in the crowded jeans market, I wanted to make Diesel an exclusive brand. My first move was to drastically reduce our distribution channels and begin opening single-brand stores. I wanted to develop the concept of exclusivity while tightly controlling the brand's image. The idea was to showcase all of our beautiful and unique products, but even more than that, to shape an entire Diesel lifestyle. Stores seemed crucial to that goal. The setting where a product is sold is key because that setting communicates a clear message about the brand.

Our first stores were in New York, London, and Rome, and they were beautiful. Each one was wholly unique, with its own identity and personality. Soon, though, we decided that we needed to create a model to use for multiple stores. We commissioned a well-known English company that conceived a store prototype, and we began opening stores based on this prototype around the world. The stores were doing well, but I wasn't happy. I myself would never have gone into one of those Diesel stores. One day, during an international meeting with all our sales and marketing managers, I took to the podium dressed as a gladiator, and I made an important announcement, saying, "Even though things are going well, I want to change everything. I want each store to have a completely different interior from the next. Also, each store should carry different products, depending on the city, the street it's located on, and its customer base." My managers hated me, but the average Diesel customer is sophisticated and loves to travel. I wanted to give them a reason to visit a Diesel store wherever they were in the world. I figured Diesel fans would do a grand tour, trying to see all of them.

To customize each store, I started buying containers full of furniture, signs, billboards, and accessories in secondhand shops around the world. And I had our own interior design office work on each store together with local architects. I didn't consult real estate agencies to choose the locations either. Instead, I tried to sniff out the trendiest neighborhoods by going to nightclubs. Discovering new, up-and-coming shopping areas had the added benefit of lower rents, and it built our reputation for being pioneers.

The result is that each time a customer enters a Diesel store, anywhere in the world, he or she has a new experience.

The Strategy of Stupid

Maybe the title of this chapter isn't an exact representation of the stupid approach in question. Stupid also plans, but stupid plans differently.

Most—though not all—big companies pick a single "best" strategy after consulting all kinds of analytical tools. Companies like Diesel plan based on intuition. Intuition is not a mere whim, but something you feel in your heart and stomach that will be good for the business. Renzo Rosso "felt" it was important to make Diesel an exclusive brand. Renzo Rosso "felt" that each Diesel store worldwide should offer a unique experience to attract sophisticated globe-trotting customers. Renzo Rosso "felt" it was better to open shops in up-and-coming neighborhoods (and that rents there would cost less). Then, in order to transmit those feelings to the entire company, he obviously had to make some plans as well. He couldn't very well close business with two thousand stores overnight or change all his retail stores at the same time (both for economic reasons and because it would be impossible on a practical level). He needed to plan the change process by deciding, for example, where in the world to start.

In short, stupid doesn't plan the spark that ignites change, but once it starts burning, it plans to implement that change.

One more thing: Renzo Rosso's choices anticipated some trends that later took hold throughout the entire fashion industry. Stupid is farsighted!

My stupid ideas

SMART MAY HAVE THE BRAINS BUT STUPID HAS THE BALLS.
/09

A New York Address

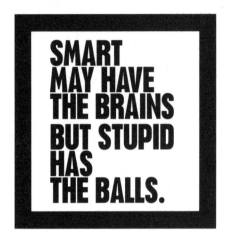

Let me tell you the story of our first store. By 1996, Diesel had become an international brand. Fashion-forward young people were buying our products, and sales were expanding rapidly in Europe and Asia. Things were going well in the United States, too, but the challenge we faced there was more difficult.

The United States was the country that had shaped my business sense, so I decided that the first store should be in New York.

It was a really competitive market, but I didn't care: The United States had inspired the dreams of my youth. America is legendary: the homeland of jeans, James Dean, rock music. Diesel had to be a part of it.

I'd long admired the Levi's brand with its status and its vintage products. I thought opening a store near the Levi's flagship would be a real challenge. Levi's had just opened its flagship store in New York, on Lexington Avenue, across the street from Bloomingdale's. So I would open mine there, too, right in front of theirs. I was so convinced that our product was high quality and unique that I didn't fear comparison. Actually, I relished the challenge. A rather stupid choice, you're probably thinking, but wait to hear the rest.

I learned that the building I had fallen in love with was about to be handed over to a big American brand. I gathered my courage, went to the office of the building's owner, and after a long series of negotiations I placed a check for one million dollars on the table. That was probably the origin of the concept of "key money" in the United States. Obviously, the owner of the building immediately agreed, and that's how we got our first store in New York.

It was total madness. The shop was fifteen thousand square feet (1,400 square meters), and I didn't have enough products to fill it with. So I created entertainment spaces—including a bar and a DJ booth—in the store. There were parties every Friday from 6 p.m. to closing time. You can imagine how much our customers loved it, but it was really something to see the faces of those who worked in the stores near us!

The staff selection was also incredible. A newspaper ad drew five hundred aspiring salespeople to a Broadway theater. Each applicant had two minutes to express him or herself in any way he or she wanted: dancing, singing, improvising, whatever. They could express themselves however they felt most comfortable. It was quite a show—a real reality show. We hired fifty-two people. I still remember the face of the fifty-second person, a young Asian woman, who burst into tears when we called her name. So we assembled a group of totally cool salespeople who didn't have a clue about how to sell merchandise.

It goes without saying that it was a huge hit.

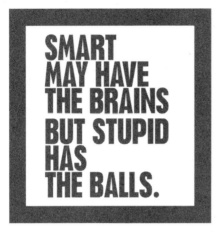

The Strategy of Stupid

In other words, stupid has courage. When a company is already strong, when it has a great team and the financial resources to try new things, and when it is closing in on its main competitor, the next question is whether to attack that competitor head-on where it lives.

This is a widely acknowledged management strategy, and there's no right or wrong answer about when it should be implemented. Of course you need courage to try. And you certainly can't do so just by imitating your competition. Renzo Rosso relied on a series of innovative elements—entertainment spaces, parties, cool staff, and much more—which made the difference and led to success.

This is one of the moments in Diesel's history that fascinates me most. I believe Italy desperately needs courageous entrepreneurs. A large number of Italian companies get ready to attack their leading international competitors, but then draw back at the last moment.

I understand the rational fear behind that hesitation. After all, going after a competitor like that makes people nervous, and rightly so. It means really shaking things up. But I'm convinced that these companies have what they *need to succeed: products, staff, financial resources. And they have to do something—if they don't make a move sooner or later, competitors will turn on them instead. Maybe all they need is a bit of "stupid" courage!*

My stupid ideas

BE STUPID. THERE'S NO WRONG WAY TO DO IT.
/10

My parents. I owe everything to them.

The day of my First Communion. Jeans had not yet entered my life.

My childhood home and my first car.

My whole career began with this sewing machine.

Diesel's first headquarters.

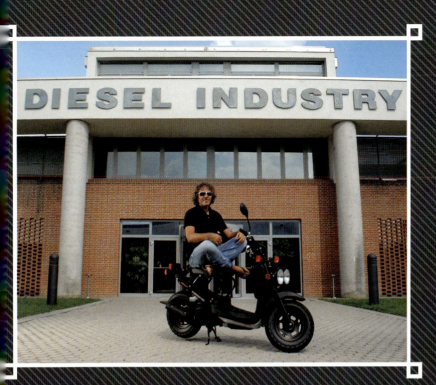

Its second headquarters.

Our current headquarters.

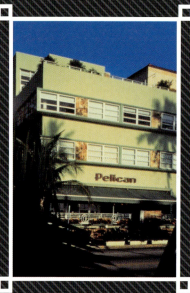
The Pelican Hotel in Miami.

The first Diesel store in NYC.

"The Daily African:" one of our most controversial ad campaigns.

Receiving the Advertiser of the Year award at Cannes in 1998: five Renzos on stage.

The great party for Diesel's big anniversary.

Only The Brave Foundation: children in the village in Mali.

Maison Martin Margiela.

Diesel Farm.

My "offsprings" Dean & Dan (Dsquared^2).

My lovely kids: Andrea, Stefano, Alessia, Luna, Asia, and India.

At Diesel.

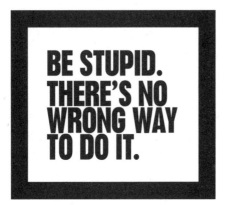

An Advertising Revolution

I've never had any patience for repetition and monotony. I always demand unique and different ideas, even for ad campaigns. I don't care if the one for this season was a big hit—next season's needs to be completely different. That's the standard by which we've judged our own ad campaigns. People always ask me which one is my favorite. I've loved all of them, but here I'll discuss the ones that amused me most because they best reflected my sense of humor.

"Super Denim" was an ad for a fake product. The commercial features a fat Indian guy with the air of a con artist. He's hawking jeans made of a synthetic fabric that he claims makes them "super resistant." It's a Bollywood film meets Jerry Lewis comedy kind of thing, really ridiculous. The first time I saw it I said, "But no one will buy our jeans!" Yet the more I watched it, the more I liked it. I figured that ridiculing what we were trying to sell would make it appealing. Another commercial is in the form of a fake American television show about "looking for Jesus." A series of clips shows people claiming they can heal the sick and walk on water. Unfortunately, the old man who is miraculously healed gets out of his wheelchair, takes two steps, and tragically falls to the ground. And the boy who tries to walk on water sinks like a stone. In the end, Jesus turns out to be an Asian guy—dressed in Diesel, naturally—who parks cars.

One of my favorites is a fake Western, where the bad guy is a fat, ugly gunman. It starts with him waking up next to . . . well, let's call her a woman of easy virtue. She's grotesquely ugly. The man throws the sheet over her head, puts on his clothes, and runs downstairs. On his way out of the saloon, he kicks a dog. Then there's a shoot-out in the street. Our good-looking hero, dressed in Diesel from head to toe, gets killed! The bad guy picks his nose and ambles away. We also invented a fake Polish country singer, Joanna. She would make public appearances and was even discussed in gossip magazines. She became so popular that we had to hire women in various countries to play her at events. I don't think any of them knew how to sing. Journalists kept asking us who Joanna really was and whether she existed at all. We even answered all her fan mail for her, signing her name to each letter. We had created the first "instant celebrity." A journalist from *Women's Wear Daily* who had written about Joanna seriously didn't speak to us for months after another journalist from the *New York Post* discovered the truth and made fun of him for falling for it.

Behind all our advertising messages lies fun—we have fun creating them, and we want others to be amused, too. Of course, it's also important to attract attention and to laugh along with our fans. At times we deal with sensitive social issues, but always with a smile on our faces.

The Strategy of Stupid

> BE STUPID. THERE'S NO WRONG WAY TO DO IT.

The commentary on this chapter isn't easy for a management expert to write. First off, I want to say that the title is incorrect because the stupid can make mistakes. At the very least, they might choose the wrong way to do something or the wrong time to do it. But maybe we should look for deeper meaning in Renzo Rosso's words. If the stupid person is the person who is able to stupefy, to amaze, to look at reality naively, then we can say that this "purity" may take many forms. And, above all, it doesn't make much sense to ask ourselves if there's a right or wrong way to amaze people. Each person is amazed and amazes others with the things that most closely match his own sensibility.

Think of art. Many people who are able to amaze themselves and others work in the world of art. When we look at a work of art, the first thing we think about isn't whether it's right or wrong, but whether we like it or not, whether it makes us feel something or not, whether it helps us see reality better. In this sense, there's no wrong way to be stupid. It doesn't seem like a coincidence to me that entrepreneurs and artists often work together very fruitfully, or even that they engage in very productive dialogue. The businessman, like a true artist, is motivated by passion. He undertakes a challenging task—trying to transmit beauty in order to draw in both customers and suitable colleagues.

But there's another thing to be learned from this chapter: more than any other business, the fashion world lets you be crazy with advertising, but of course, there's room for creativity in every industry. The important thing is to want it and not to stop innovating after one good campaign or one moment of success.

My stupid ideas

SMART HAD ONE GOOD IDEA, AND THAT WAS STUPID.
/11

Attack of the Clones

Advertising takes teamwork. As I've already written, Diesel doesn't have just one creative guru. Instead, we have a whole team. I'm a part of that team, and our ad agencies become part of the team when they work with us.

Over the years, our ad campaigns have won many awards in different countries, including many Grand Prix, Gold and Silver Lions from the International Advertising Festival in Cannes. In 1998, we were nominated for Advertiser of the Year, one of the most coveted awards in the advertising world. I always strive to give credit to all the people who work with and for us. So, the moment I found out we had won and that I was due to accept the prize, I immediately began considering what to do.

The idea that that award was being presented to me alone made me a little uneasy because I knew perfectly well that many people had contributed to our success. That's when I had an idea.

I hired a movie makeup artist from London to come and create five rubber masks of my face. I gave one to each of the four most important creative team members, and we left for Cannes to accept the award. We were all dressed alike. When the host called my name, we all went onstage, one after the other, from different directions, creating havoc. We gave the festival director, the staff, and even the audience something to see! Then I took off my mask and introduced each member of my team. This was my way of saying that the award wasn't just mine and acknowledging the value of the people who work with me.

> **SMART HAD ONE GOOD IDEA, AND THAT WAS STUPID.**

The Strategy of Stupid

This is one of the best examples of managerial talent—even though Renzo Rosso might not like that expression—in this book. Just image what those four team members were thinking when they got on stage in Cannes with Rosso. After a memorable experience like that, where they all shared in the success, how could they fail to give their best to a person who had the intelligence, sensitivity, and courage to shout from the rooftops that his team members are key? Think, too, of the effect this must have had on other executives of the company. The entrepreneur shared his success onstage for all to see. How could some other manager now take credit for other people's work? That evening, Renzo Rosso indelibly created a special atmosphere within his company.

I've seen many businessmen win awards for many reasons. Some—though not many—didn't even bother mentioning that others contributed to the success recognized with those awards. At most, they mentioned their families. Still others—again, not many—mentioned their coworkers with such detachment that it read like an obligation. Many others rightly thanked their colleagues profusely. But few have taken the time to ask themselves,

"How can I make everyone, both inside and outside the company, understand that we really are a team?" Rosso asked himself that question, and he landed on a solution that was truly original. Or, as he would say, truly stupid!

My stupid ideas

SMART SAYS NO. STUPID SAYS YES.
/12

Risk and Reward

Allow me to say another thing about advertising. I'd like to tell you a story about the importance of staying true to your own ideas.

In 2001 we conceived of an ad campaign titled "The Daily African." It was based on a simple yet decidedly provocative idea. The photos portrayed Africans in over-the-top lavish settings: the steps of a villa, a library lined with shelves of books, the backseat of a limo. They had all the trappings of photographs of rich Americans in their country homes, but they featured Africans dressed completely in Diesel.

The photos were accompanied by cutouts from the imaginary newspaper *The Daily African*, and the content of the articles was quite different from the news that normally comes out of African countries. The headlines read, "Africa agrees on financial aid to America," and "African expedition to explore unknown Europe by foot," as well as "Birthrate booms in Italy and Spain. Europe set back even further," "African hostages free after being held for 148 days by Californian rebels," "African Union space program meets criticism for plans to use Europeans in intergalactic travel," and so on.

Preconceived notions of Africa, all totally overturned, in true Diesel style. And yet, we had doubts about the campaign! Would the African-American community find it disrespectful? And how would Africans react? Maybe everyone would be offended! We started second-guessing ourselves and wondering whether this time we had gone too far.

Despite our indecision, we kept being drawn to the photos; they just felt special. There was only one way to find out if they would work, so we showed the campaign to three editors of very influential magazines: Ingrid Sischy at *Interview*, Kim Hastreiter at *Paper*, and Emil Wilbekin at *Vibe*.

The response was astonishing. They all deemed the campaign absolutely innovative, direct, courageous, respectful, intelligent, and, above all, funny. So we put it out there.

As usual, we caused a stir. Debate broke out in newspapers. Surprisingly, however, most people thought our campaign humorously challenged common prejudice in the media and public opinion about Africa.

It quickly became one of our most praised ad campaigns ever. It even won the Grand Prix at Cannes. Of course, that wasn't our first award, but I was thrilled that "The Daily African" had been picked as the best ad campaign in the world, beating out thousands of others!

That same year, we changed our historical agency. I really can't help being stupid.

The Strategy of Stupid

When dealing with an engineer who wants to research a radically innovative production process, a designer who comes up with an idea for a totally original product, or an advertising agent who proposes an extremely provocative campaign, a businessman may ask for the process, the product, or the campaign to be toned down in order to make it less risky.

In a normal situation, that just isn't reasonable, unless, of course, the engineer, designer, or advertising agent is acting rashly. A businessman should be aware that such things are carefully considered before they are submitted to him, and he shouldn't try to alter them drastically. Really, the only two reasonable responses are to decline and say no, or to accept the proposal and begin investing.

Radical innovation underlies a company's long-term success.

That's why no entrepreneur should say no to change proposed by his own employees too frequently. What he can and must do is avoid climbing high, only to fall.

The idea of asking three trusted, nonconformist, and trend-conscious magazine editors—people who don't mind walking the line between provocative and scandalous—for their opinions on the ad campaign "The Daily African" was both stupid and useful in order to understand *whether it went too far or not. Stupid-intelligents try to understand—even if it means checking with others—how to say yes so that they don't have to pass up a brilliant idea.*

My stupid ideas

FRIENDS/02

We're with stupid . . .

TO BE STUPID

TO BE FUNNY

TO BE UNIQUE

TO BE FREE

TO BE REAL

OR JUST TO BE

CAN BE STUPID

TO STAND UP FOR YOUR RIGHTS

CAN BE STUPID

GOING AGAINST THE GRAIN

CAN BE STUPID

WHAT'S LIFE FOR

IF YOU CAN'T BE STUPID!

TO BE STUPID CAN ALSO

BE CONSIDERED BEING BRAVE

LIKE OUR DEAR FRIEND

MISTER RR!

"ONLY THE BRAVE"

THE STUPID RISK TAKER

CHANGING THE WAYS OF LIFE

THANK YOU FOR BEING STUPID:
AND CHANGING OUR LIVES!

Dean and Dan Caten
Designers of DSquared²

ARE YOU SMART ENOUGH TO BE STUPID? /13

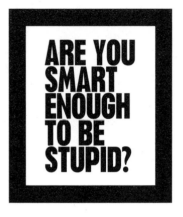

Technology is My Playground

I've always been fascinated by technology. In the 1980s I had the dashboard of my car altered and a button installed that could open the gate at the headquarters and at my home and turn on the lights in my yard! I even had a car phone back then. It was a gigantic box. And in 1990 I was one of the first lucky people who got a trial cell phone during the World Cup. It was a slightly smaller box, but you still needed a bag to carry it around! When it comes to my company, too, I've always bought the latest technology: much innovative CAD-CAM technology (CAD-CAM stands for Computer Aided Design and Computer Aided Manufacturing; it's the software used both to develop garments and to manufacture them—in layman's terms, it allows you to make patterns with a computer) was developed in our offices by our engineers and manufacturing experts.

In 1995, we launched our Web site, and it sparked a revolution. We were the first fashion brand to have an Internet presence, and it didn't even feature our products! During those years in the United States people started selling all kinds of things online so I thought we should also have an online store. I chose Switzerland as a pilot country because we found a company there that guaranteed delivery of orders within twenty-four hours. Today that sounds normal, but at the time delivery took as long as three or four days—sometimes even a whole week. We sold our core product—jeans—but only a small selection of styles. It was fascinating to see how many people—meaning how few—came to the site every day, what they chose, and the questions they asked. I remember I was on cloud nine when we sold sixteen pairs of jeans in one day.

From an economic point of view, an online store didn't make much sense back then. But I believe you should always stay one step ahead of everyone else. Now our online business represents a large chunk of our sales, and we've entrusted it to a specialized partner, Yoox.

Today the Web is an increasingly important communication and business tool for Diesel, and it is catalyzing our investments. I like the Web because it is democratic and transparent and allows you to communicate directly with others. It is also the place for a young, curious, and informed audience. It allows us to interact with our fans around the world, place our messages on social networks and poke fun at ourselves, and it lets our fans do the same. My love for gadgets may seem childish, but it has helped my company grow.

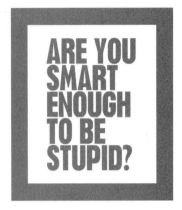

The Strategy of Stupid

"From an economic point of view an online store didn't make much sense back then. But I believe you should always stay one step ahead of everyone else." An entrepreneur cannot hesitate to invest in the future because sooner or later it will become clear that some of these investments convey a competitive advantage.

The three forms of investment that seem most likely to create a lasting advantage for many Italian companies are investments in brands, new markets, and technology.

Renzo Rosso has done well in all three categories. He isn't afraid of technology. He embraces it enthusiastically and tries to be an early adopter, as well as encouraging his colleagues to use it.

Obviously, early adopters run a risk because early technology is still being tested. On the other hand, they have the great advantage of being the first to assess the potential of such technology, and they don't find themselves caught off guard when it becomes mainstream.

It's no coincidence that Diesel invested first and more than others in the Web. This tool knocks down barriers inside and outside the company. You can communicate directly with consumers. But above all, young people much prefer to communicate electronically, and young people are *at the heart of Diesel's strategy. Any delay in adopting this technology would have seriously undermined the brand's reputation.*

My stupid ideas

STUPID IS TRIAL AND ERROR. MOSTLY ERROR.

/14

The Time Things Went Poorly

Being stupid doesn't mean being successful all of the time. In the late 1980s, I started to open branches in a few other large countries. In 1993, I decided to open a branch in Buenos Aires, Argentina, because it was considered (by me) a strategic center of South America. I bought a marvelous building in Boca (only to discover many years later that half of the building I loved, including the facade, had already been sold to the city of Buenos Aires) to open a showroom that would serve not just Argentina, but all of Latin America. We even opened three stores in Buenos Aires.

Despite our best efforts, we were never able to develop the business in a rational and profitable way. Since Argentina's seasons are the opposite of those in North America, they had to purchase merchandise with an eye to selling the products six months later. Plus, the economy wasn't great. The dramatic crash came shortly afterward. For the first time, I was forced to close a branch, even though I had wanted it so badly.

Another "unsuccess" story was the license I signed with a big American business. In the late 1980s, Diesel was beginning to be considered cool, and it was customary during those years to license your brand and have products carrying your brand name produced and sold in local markets. We were all enthusiastic because we wanted to create something big, but it proved complex to transfer our background, our vibe, and our passion for a very new and different product to our partner. They just didn't get it. At that time, the United States was totally marketing driven, and it was hard to explain our products' innovative features. Our partner started to create a much simpler product so they could set lower prices than their competition. The result was a hybrid product that didn't have the quality of the original. After just two years, the partnership was dissolved. I thought I was signing on with a great partner in a great big country, and that that would automatically spell success. What I didn't get was that the product I wanted to make was more than simply a product of business: It had a soul that couldn't be bought and sold.

I've made many stupid mistakes in my life, but fortunately they've always helped me to learn, to grow, and to add to my experiences.

The Strategy of Stupid

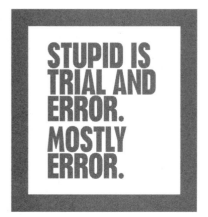

I wholeheartedly agree with Renzo Rosso: *mistakes can lead to success for a person and a company.*

A young entrepreneur who successfully managed to grow his company once told me, "There are three elements needed for successful growth: leadership, or the ability to guide; experience; and bad experience. In fact, bad experience is a necessary part of a success story. Of course, you need to be strong enough to pick up the pieces and start over again."

The best companies aren't those that never make mistakes (only those who never try never fail) and maybe not even those that make fewer mistakes than others. They're the ones that immediately recognize their mistakes and turn to seeking a solution. If they can't find one, the experience is over and they accept failure. They have the strength to start over again, heading in another direction.

You need to be humble to see your own mistakes. It takes courage to accept loss. In order to start over, you need personality, good morale. All qualities that the stupid person has and that each of us can develop if we try to look at reality with the attitude of a "loser" who has more to *learn than to teach. As a university professor, I know how hard it is to have that attitude! But it's worth it, in the long run.*

My stupid ideas

HELLO STUPID. GOODBYE PANTS. /15

Nights (and Days) with the Heidis

When low-waist pants were the hottest trend, I had a vision. Instead of hiding your underwear under your clothes, why not use it as a means of communication—of oneself, of one's personality—and seduction? Underwear, a category dominated for years by Calvin Klein, could be more than basic black or white; it could be enlivened with colors, patterns, designs. We could use the same concept we applied to T-shirts, but this time for something that was usually hidden. Why not create interest, evoke a lifestyle, and seduce a partner even during the act of undressing? Our underwear was a huge success, and as is often the case, we changed the way people saw something—in this case, underwear.

The easy thing would have been to take famous soccer players or top models and photograph them in all their statuary beauty while wearing our products. But we're stupid.

We hired two young women—we called both Heidi—and we invented a story about them "kidnapping" Juan, our underwear salesperson. They stole the collections and held him hostage for a week in a hotel room as they tried on the products. The room was in fact a television studio like the one used for the filming of *Big Brother*. There were eight video cameras turned on 24/7, connected to our diesel.com site, which also had been "hijacked" by the young women. This was during the first social network boom: the two Heidis used MySpace and YouTube to broadcast their message and show videos and photos of the "prison." Viewers were invited to vote on which torment both of them would inflict on Juan—things like waxing his legs or putting ice cubes in his underwear. All these pranks could be seen on the Web site, and the funniest scenes were regularly posted on YouTube.

At the end of the week, my son Stefano entered the hotel room to free Juan, who didn't seem too happy that his adventure was coming to an end. But Stefano was forced to strip down to his underwear as well and promise the Heidis an ad contract!

This new type of communication snowballed. Once again the marketing world acknowledged us for our innovation and ability to combine popular trends—*Big Brother*, social networks—with brand communication.

The Strategy of Stupid

This chapter introduces two themes. One is using the media, such as social networks, to which young people gravitate. This we've already discussed. The second is expanding in a parallel way, in this case, into the underwear category. The strategy for parallel growth is simple: after achieving success in one field, companies move into other similar or related sectors.

Many successful fashion companies have tried their hand at this kind of parallel growth, but it does have its risks: you could dilute the brand value by getting into an area that doesn't have much in common with the original one; you may find that the competition is different in the new area. The great advantage of this kind of expansion is that you probably already have some resources that you can put to good use (in Diesel's case, a well-known brand, communications expertise, and a solid distribution network). Most importantly, you stop the company from falling into a state of inertia. Sooner or later, a successful business rests on its laurels. Parallel expansion forces companies to muster renewed energy as they pursue success all over again with a new product.

Diesel followed this strategy with an appropriate method: it entered a related market and did so with an innovative communications strategy in order to stand out *from the crowd. Above all, it never neglected its original focus, since that was still the source of most of its earnings and profit.*

My stupid ideas

FRIENDS/03

Dear Renzo,

One morning thousands and thousands of years ago, some bearded guy dressed in a fur returned to his cave, rolling a tree trunk in front of himself. He announced that rolling things was useful. They told him he was stupid and advised him not to wander too far from the cave or some hungry animal that was faster than he was would surely eat him.

You're in good company, Renzo. They told Christopher Columbus that if he sailed in that direction, he would fall off the planet or encounter a monster that ate stupid people.

You are perhaps even more "stupid" than Christopher Columbus. He discovered America, and you discovered that things can be rediscovered, time and time again. You did that using the worldwide symbol of rebellion, freedom, equality, individuality: A PAIR OF JEANS.

Jeans already existed, and they were American, a symbol of the influence of American values in the free and freed world. You reinvented them, and you made people in their homeland, the United States, see them with new eyes. You're stupid, Renzo! How could you ever dare to think that you could sell jeans to Americans?

Every time I travel the world and see the Diesel brand somewhere—and it's just about everywhere—I think about possibilities. But I also feel stupid like you. The world needs stupid people, with stupid ideas like yours.

Stupid sees things that aren't there, while others call him stupid. But those things really are there. You just need to draw them out with passion, talent, and hard work because sometimes being stupid isn't enough.

When I first saw a BE STUPID billboard, I was riding my bike. I stopped and paid tribute to you with a great big smile.

Good job, Renzo. You've done it again. In just two words, you've expressed the age in which we live.

Your friend Lorenzo "Jova," aspiring stupid
(Lorenzo Cherubini,
Italian songwriter, singer, and rapper)

BE STUPID. YOU'LL MAKE MORE FRIENDS.
/16

Teamwork

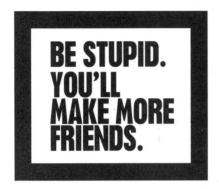

The biggest mistake you can make is to think you can do something all alone. My career has spanned more than thirty years, and I still dedicate a lot of time to choosing partners and colleagues. And I still want to learn what I don't know from others.

One of my favorite lines from the "Be Stupid" campaign is "Smart recognizes things for how they are. Stupid sees things for how they could be." I often keep that in mind when hiring, and some of the people I hired based on that philosophy have gone on to have incredible careers. I've always been convinced of two things. The first is that hungry people are more determined and motivated than the successful ones. That's why I often look for the number twos. They're often hiding behind their bosses, but they are the ones doing the job: they know this and would like to shine on their own. My second belief, supported by my personal experience, is that there are people who are intrinsically worth more than their titles and more than what they've accomplished up to that point would indicate. One of many examples: I hired a cool guy I met in a gas station and made him my salesperson for Germany—he became so successful he gave me a Porsche! I also hired a character from Italy's historical telecommunications company and made him my first communications director; we raked in our first Lions together at the advertising festival in Cannes. In the mid-1990s, I was the first person in fashion to hire executives from large-scale corporations, such as Danone, Proctor & Gamble, and Unilever.

Was it easy? No. Was it stupid? It seemed so, at the time. Did it work? Almost always! Fashion was the only field I knew well, yet once we started to think big, I recognized almost immediately that most of the people working in fashion were fairly mediocre. I was fascinated by Americans and especially by American businesses. I contacted international headhunters and told them what I was looking for. Luckily, I found some headhunters who were as stupid as I was. They began introducing me to people who would never have been on my radar; the candidates must have been wondering what they were doing there! It was a revelation. Needless to say, at first it was challenging. My longtime colleagues would say, "What in the world does this guy know about denim or lifestyle? He sells toothpaste and snack food!" The newcomers—accustomed to strict market analysis and different professional standards—told me we were doing everything wrong and that we had to change the entire organization. They wanted to alter the company's DNA, which I had spent so many years cultivating, in the hope of achieving higher sales. One day I came in to find ten resignation letters on my desk! I started to cry. What in the world had I done? But it's often the case that your vision is clearest during a crisis, and that's how it all turned out for me at the time.

Ultimately, we ended up with a company and a corporate group with the added values of passion and professionalism—a winning combination. Today, my team continues to amaze me and make me proud. When I look at other companies, even companies that are bigger and more structured than ours, I can't help but think how fortunate I've been to work with my team.

BE STUPID. YOU'LL MAKE MORE FRIENDS.

The Strategy of Stupid

This chapter begins with a great truth: "The biggest mistake you can make is to think you can do something all alone." Entrepreneurs need to be aware of this before their companies can grow and move forward. Without that awareness, they won't delegate responsibility and they won't attract high-performing executives.

This chapter makes a number of other pertinent points—some of them about the fashion business, and others about business in general. One of those is that companies need new managers, including people from outside the field, who bring new experiences with them. You also have to ask people who have worked with you for some time to get reenergized. But more than anything, I'm amazed by Renzo Rosso's description of the large amount of time he has dedicated to teaching insider and outsider managers to work together. He really pushed to integrate newcomers from other industries and companies with his longtime colleagues. Many businesspeople focus all their energy on products and the market; others focus on manufacturing processes. Still others dedicate attention to the economic/financial side of things. I believe it would benefit the business world greatly if more businesspeople spent more time in contact with people—speaking to them and letting them speak. It's important for everyone to have a role to play. If you don't do this work, you may fail to notice that people are at profit levels that can't be sustained, or you may be unintentionally creating an atmosphere that feels precarious, and we all know how that ends up. I know Rosso didn't write this book because he wanted to teach readers a lesson. But this chapter deserves to be studied closely—it is stupefying.

My stupid ideas

BE STUPID. YOU'LL CREATE MORE.
/17

Diesel Gets into High Fashion

In the 1990s, the luxury market began to expand: famous brands grew and it seemed that customers were willing to spend more and more on exclusive products. I was attracted to the luxury market business model, which is basically to produce less, but to bet on quality.

At Diesel, this meant making very limited numbers of treated jeans, each pair unique. We were pioneers in so-called "premium denim." That was such a success that I thought we should take things one step further and create a cutting-edge line of products for our most demanding consumers, who loved the idea of exclusivity. So we launched a brand extension called DieselStyleLab, which, as the name indicates, was truly an experimental design lab.

In order to create this line, I looked for a high-end fashion company with a lot of know-how when it came to making products with Italian craftsmanship. I needed a company that could create well-crafted, tailored garments. I learned of Staff International, which was already producing collections for brands such as Vivienne Westwood, Ungaro, Missoni, Costume National, Karl Lagerfeld, and Maison Martin Margiela. Actually, they were almost like tailors: discreet, precise craftsmen who worked behind the scenes.

But despite the high quality of its work, Staff International was going through some tough times. Indeed, the company was on the verge of bankruptcy. But it had begun doing excellent work for DieselStyleLab, and I didn't want to see it close its doors. So, in 1999, I decided to buy the company. That marked my entry into a world that was completely new to me: the world of ready-to-wear and fashion.

In taking over Staff International, I could have gone the conventional route and let the company go into bankruptcy proceedings, which would have allowed me to buy it without shouldering its debt and without the redundant personnel. Instead, I took the stupid route. I took it upon myself to reorganize and relaunch a valueless company whose know-how could have disappeared. I still recall the day I acquired the company: the employees were perplexed and apprehensive. They probably wondered how someone who had only worked with jeans could make this high fashion company grow. The atmosphere was difficult, even hostile at times. The ready-to-wear world had always looked down on the casual world. So I focused on restructuring the company by ushering in freshness, innovation, and managerial expertise. I tried to combine my knowledge of denim with their tailoring expertise. I chose to keep some brands and let go of others, namely the brands that I didn't think in line with my vision of future fashion. I also brought in a new brand that would later prove to be a great investment: DSquared², a "bridge" brand between my world and the world of Staff International. This marked the creation of one of the major niches in fashion today: luxury casual.

Through Staff International, I discovered a whole new world of intriguing designers and had the opportunity to get to know Maison Martin Margiela, a very unusual fashion house famous for its minimalist clothing, considered so avant-garde and experimental that it bordered on art. Its founder, Martin Margiela, was an enigmatic figure: he refused to give interviews or be photographed, even though the high-fashion world thrived on personality and the charisma of designers. Martin was a real genius, and his work challenged conventional ideas about clothing. He came up with items that were created by taking apart vintage garments and sewing their parts back together, a clever reinterpretation of the classics.

I was flattered the day he came and asked me if I was interested in becoming his partner and in helping him develop his line. Obviously, I accepted. I found out later that, even though he had already received invitations to partner with some of the biggest groups in fashion, Martin chose me because he understood that he would be free to develop and carry out his vision.

In 2002 I started working with Martin, a unique figure, a true artist in every sense, with a really different vision that could be applied to various fields. For each problem I had, he would—in a matter of minutes, with confidence and charm—find a solution, and it was always well-suited and visionary. We started to bring managerial techniques and technology to the company, and we developed various product lines —from clothing to accessories—that, taken as a whole, depicted Margiela's universe: white, unique, and offbeat. We launched these items in new single-brand stores. But things weren't easy with the maison: I wanted to introduce modern strategies to grow the brand, but at the same time preserve its spirit and originality. This meant that it took longer to restructure the company, but in the end I could be really proud of the results. It was worth it because through that kind of development, the maison managed to raise its profile. At the same time, I earned the respect of the fashion world. I still believe today that young designers who want to develop their talents consider it the best place to work.

Luckily, I had Martin with me right from the start, helping me to make the entire Maison more efficient. He was the one responsible for this innovation.

Martin has recently decided to retire and leave the fashion world in order to dedicate himself to art and traveling. I admire him greatly, and I continue to admire and respect his choices.

In 2003, we created Only The Brave, the holding company that today manages Diesel, Maison Martin Margiela, Staff International, and the newly acquired Viktor & Rolf.

In the meantime, Diesel has launched its first line, Diesel Black Gold, a premium version of the Diesel lifestyle. All brands under the Only The Brave umbrella represent my vision of "new luxury."

The Strategy of Stupid

At some point in a company's history, one must decide whether to confidently enter related fields. Renzo Rosso was successful with underwear, so it was only natural for him to start thinking about other opportunities. But he followed the road less traveled. First, he looked for a ready-to-wear company to create his more exclusive Diesel line; then, seeing that his chosen company had fallen on hard times, he decided to buy it rather than switching to another one. What's more, he didn't buy it during bankruptcy proceedings, which would mean losing precious know-how. Instead, he reorganized it himself, thinking long-term. After having restructured the company, he humbled himself as he was exposed to a whole new world, so he was able to "listen to" people—such as Martin Margiela— who had experience in that sector. In turn, he shared his own knowledge of technology, management, and product strategy. Why did Martin and Renzo become friends? Maybe because Rosso didn't show off his intelligence or his money. Maybe because he didn't criticize the maison's shortcomings.

A sharp financial analyst could tell you whether currently the Only The Brave brands, excluding Diesel, are producing good results. But stupid is probably more interested in the fact that if Diesel hadn't gone down this path, it would never have learned all about ready-to-wear. Diversification can help a family-run business diminish risk, especially over the long term.

My stupid ideas

BE STUPID. YOU'LL NEVER WANT TO BE ANYWHERE ELSE.
/18

The First Fashion Hotel

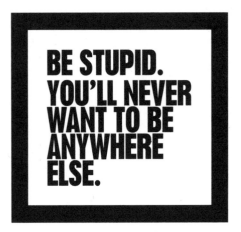

On my way to the Caribbean, where I was going on research for a collection inspired by the sea and the tropics, I stopped in Miami with my designer friend Reny. We went to South Beach, and I was amazed by the architecture and design in this small, decaying neighborhood along the ocean. At the time, the Art Deco buildings on Ocean Drive were falling to pieces. The only people living there were retirees who came to escape the cold up north.

Yet the setting was magical: the light was incredible and made this an ideal location for fashion shoots. I was mesmerized by this curious combination of old buildings, elderly people, gorgeous models, and the beach. I realized this was a place that was ripe for development. Maybe this was a good time to invest.

I fell in love with one building in particular: the Pelican Hotel, built in 1933. Forty-eight hours later, the hotel was mine. When I got back to Italy, my CEO was furious with me for making such a hasty investment. And on the other side of the world! Even my American colleagues told me the idea was totally wrong-headed, that Americans all looked down on Miami and thought of it as a city full of criminals and illegal immigrants. No American would ever vacation in South Beach, they told me.

I had faith in my stupid idea. I firmly believed South Beach had the potential to become a hot vacation spot, and not only for Americans. The beach was just too beautiful and the people were just too fascinating for it not to work. So I decided to create an unconventional, welcoming hotel where guests would feel at home. There were no hotels like that in Miami back then. I shared my idea with my creative team, and we were all excited about it. We furnished each room differently, assigning each one a different theme. A brilliant idea, but I needed someone who could see the project through.

I settled on Magnus, who at the time sold jeans in Sweden and had contributed to the interior design of our Swedish office. He had a wacky style, and just as wacky was my idea to send him to Miami for two years to oversee the work on the Pelican. I explained to him what I had in mind: I wanted to create the first fashion hotel.

It had to be a special place, where each room was unique. Guests would ask themselves, "Who do I want to be tonight?" or the reception staff would ask, "What kind of mood are you in today?" Then guests could choose the rooms most suited to the way they felt. At the Pelican there's the minimalist room, the industrial room, the hi-tech room. Some rooms look like brothels.

173

Others are psychedelic or reflect different time periods. Whatever your mood, one of the twenty-seven rooms and suites is right for you. (I even built my own personal getaway on the top floor.)

At that point I needed a hotel director. A friend of mine managed a small restaurant in Bassano. He had two key qualities: he knew everything there was to know about food and he knew how to entertain guests. I had the stupid idea of sending him to Miami. He would have to change his life completely. He would need to sell his restaurant and dedicate himself to managing something one hundred times more complex, with all the problems that would entail, using a language he didn't speak.

Today it's not unusual to move to another country for work, but twenty years ago, when we couldn't communicate as easily, thinking about "shipping" people to another part of the world was sheer madness. I wanted the Pelican to communicate the Diesel philosophy and my lifestyle. I wanted it to feel like a family business that dealt with customers with kindness and developed relationships with them. Actually, that idea underlies everything I've done in my life. Over the course of just a few years, the Pelican was being called one of the top fifty boutique hotels in the world and it was a sought-after destination.

The hotel opened in 1993 and was admittedly the first fashion hotel. Since we opened the Pelican, all the other hotels on Ocean Drive have been renovated, and South Beach has indeed become a very popular vacation destination for people around the world, especially Americans. The whole area is completely different from how it was when people called me stupid for buying a hotel there.

The Strategy of Stupid

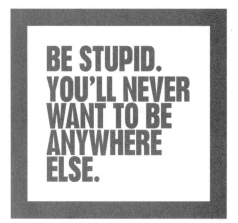

In addition to underwear and ready-to-wear, the opportunity to run a hotel presents itself. The "stupid" entrepreneur never stops and never backs down from any challenge.

And the ingredients are always the same: the impulse to try something new, love for an old building in an area that hasn't yet been recognized (which translates into saving on investment costs), a proposal for radical innovation (a fashion hotel), a crazy Swedish collaborator (Magnus, who agreed to uproot his life), a friend who's an expert in hospitality (the restaurant owner from Bassano, who also agreed to give up everything and change his life), and the reliance on a lifestyle based on a friendly attitude and connecting with others.

Maybe it's this very ability to unite solid traditional values—like friendship and kindness—and radical modern ideas—like a whole new notion of hospitality—that has made the Pelican Hotel such a success. It may even be behind the success of Renzo Rosso and the Diesel lifestyle in general. If you don't stay up-to-date, you can't hope to speak to a contemporary population—especially young people—but without tradition you lose the ability to make people feel comfortable—to make them feel at *home. Without both of those things, you'll never build a community inside and outside the company.*

That very community underpins Diesel's long-term success.

My stupid ideas

FAMILY

You Are Born and Grow Stupid

Our family has always been close. We all share certain strong values and emotions from our farming roots and simple upbringing. But the great thing is that these values combine with a unique, international, and open-minded way of seeing the world, irreverently and with a strong sense of humor—in short, stupid!

When we were young our parents took us to our grandparents' almost every summer. We couldn't wait to get there. And we did a lot of stupid things once we did. We'd sneak into the parking lot and start the tractor, or we'd jump into the corn silo, or we'd drive our grandfather's small car, a Fiat 126, around the fields.

But our childhood wasn't exactly ordinary. We spent a lot of time at Diesel. When we were kids, we even napped on top of jeans piled in bins while our parents worked. We often invented games to pass the time, like rolling down hills made of jeans or building houses out of cardboard boxes held together with tape.

This ongoing contact with the company allowed us to see things at a younger age than many people do, and it left us very open toward "the other." It's pretty unusual to have parents who take you to clubs to see fashion shows when you're ten years old, or who constantly have strange people with hair of all colors and lengths hanging around the house, or who take you on intercontinental trips to exotic places to visit manufacturing sites, calling them vacations! Maybe that's why each of us, after graduating, went abroad: we wanted to express our natural inclination to be STUPID.

You're born STUPID. And we were lucky because we lived in the ideal setting for it.

But you can also become STUPID, if you have the courage to change and do things differently and to veer from what fate seems to have in store for you. That's the definition of being visionary—seeing things as they could be instead of how they are.

These are the most important things our parents taught us, and we'll never be able to thank them enough.

BE FREE, BE BRAVE, BE STUPID

Andrea, Stefano, and Alessia Rosso
Renzo's children

STUPID IS GOOD FOR YOU.

Our Foundation

I'm convinced that a businessman must always give something back: to his employees, to his clients, and to the world in general.

That's why I've always gotten involved in humanitarian projects, especially on a local level and far away from the spotlight. I've never boasted of my involvement; I've preferred to be discreet.

Then, one day, I met His Holiness the Dalai Lama. He said to me, "You should make the most of your name! People know who you are, so your name has power. You can attract the attention of people who will want to help you."

He advised me to structure my various charity activities more rigorously. "You're a businessman," he said. "Your job is to make money, so concentrate on that. But you need a team of people who can help you to use that money for others well."

So I created the Only The Brave Foundation, a not-for-profit organization born to mobilize and empower youth to end extreme poverty. The foundation works on economic development, education, and health issues. We don't spend a lot on administration, so we really use the money to help people.

Right now we invest 10 percent in the area where we are based. It goes to computers for schools, sports teams for children, and local events; we also aid needy families, not with financial assistance, but through job creation. The rest we spend abroad. Currently, our biggest project involves helping a community of twenty thousand people in Mali that will soon become entirely self-sufficient, with schools, farms, healthcare facilities, and sports facilities. As you can imagine, I'm quite excited about this. I personally went to Mali to visit the village, and I'm working with people there to offer my experience in implementing this project. I hope it will become a social development model that communities around the world can use in order to achieve living conditions that are similar to those of more developed countries.

I've received a lot of good advice. Bono from U2 once told me, "Governments don't have enough money to support all humanitarian organizations. It's up to businessmen."

People like Bono and Steve Jobs are great at communicating, and that's how they're able to accomplish so much. I, too, want to play my part.

I dream of giving my own "stupid" contribution to making the world a better place.

CONCLUSION
THERE'S NO CURE FOR STUPID

Long after the "Be Stupid" advertising campaign is over, the philosophy behind it will remain in Diesel's DNA. We find it impossible to stop trying, testing, and experimenting because that is simply what we do. Reading some of the stories again, it occurs to me that being stupid has a way of working out. Rather like a disastrous vacation that becomes a delightful adventure in the retelling, a stupid decision often seems like a good idea once the dust has settled. A homemade pair of jeans can inspire a young man to do better. An oversized store can force its owners to try out a new kind of retailing. An untested advertising agency can create a campaign that changes the way people see fashion. An unconventional approach to sponsorship can turn out to be a way of nurturing talent. And the impulse purchase of a dilapidated hotel can lead to a unique travel experience.

Another key lesson from this book concerns the way we recruit staff. Looking back, it is clear that we hardly ever hire an employee in a conventional way. Often, we take them out of an environment in which they feel secure and put them down in another, where they have little experience, just to see what they will do. Inevitably, their innocence leads them to do things differently. And the result is often quite magical.

To "Be Stupid" is to be open to possibility. It is to embrace the possibility of failure, to walk off the map, to ignore the small voice of reason, and heed the call of crazy.

To "Be Stupid" is to take a leap of faith. Having read about one company's growth, by trial and error, I hope you'll be inspired in your own work. I am by no means advocating recklessness—to "Be Stupid" is not to commit suicide, either literally or financially. I am simply saying that innovation does not come by playing it safe.

The road is long, and there are many opportunities to make the smart choice. Try to avoid them.

Enjoy xxx,
                             RR

ACKNOWLEDGMENTS

I would like to thank a few of the people who have made this publication possible: Professor Guido Corbetta, who, without ever having met me, agreed to provide some objective, academic commentary on the history and adventures of a stupid person before his time; Antonella Viero, for having refreshed my memories and helped me to write them in a style that tells readers who I truly am; my son Stefano, for having overseen this project with passion, humbleness, and genuine curiosity to understand, explain, and learn something new about us and our history.

And, finally, I would like to thank all the people I've encountered along the way, who have inspired me to be stupid, who have allowed me and pushed me to make stupid choices, and who have encouraged me to be the most stupid of them all.

For Successful Living,
Renzo Rosso

Special thanks to Arianna Alessi